Moms and

Mom is a bus driver.

SCHOOL

Dad is a window cleaner.

Mom is a police officer.

Dad is a vet.

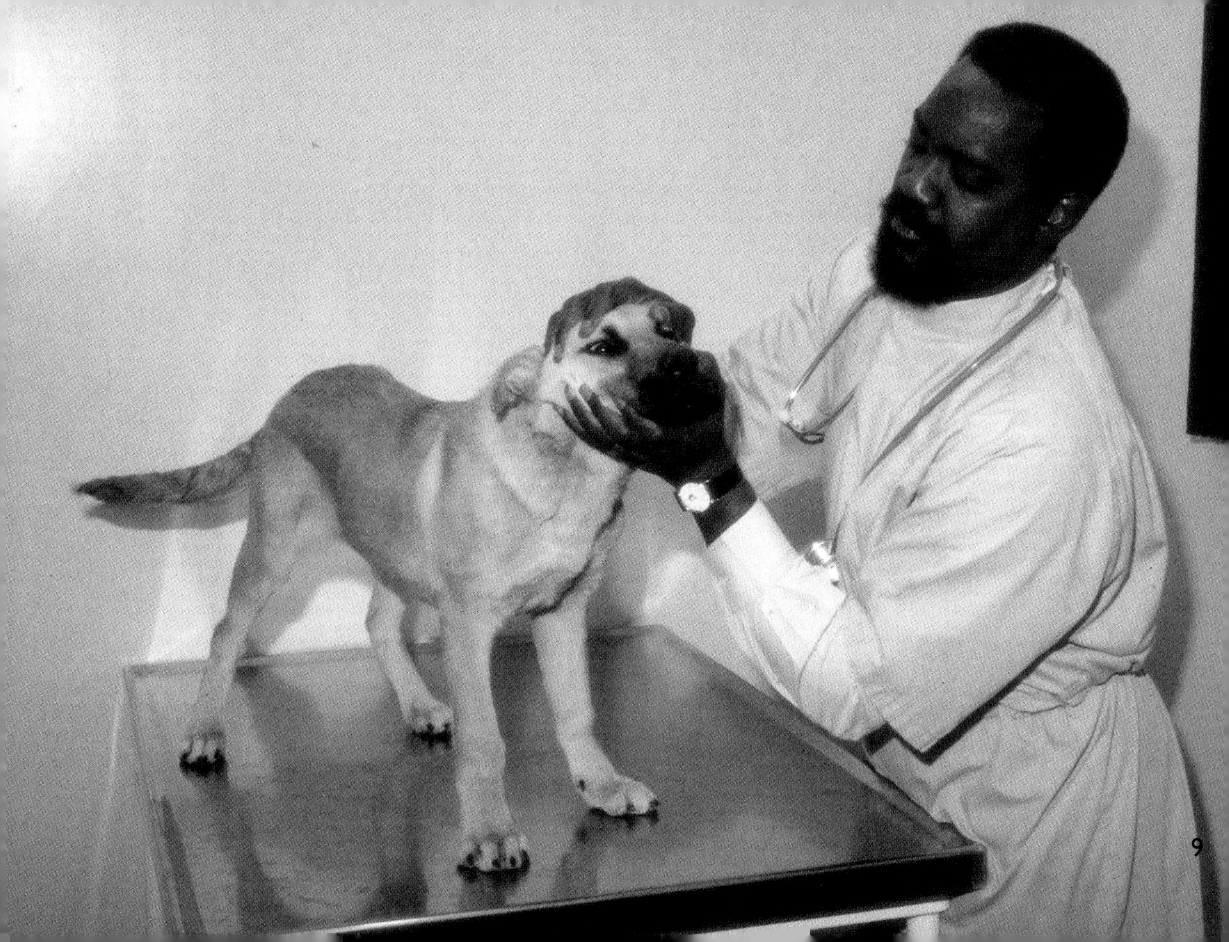

Mom is a librarian.

The Troll in the Hole
Gene Zion
By PAT HUTCHINS
At The Café Splendid
Open the Door
Eric Carle
The Very Busy Spider
Find Me a Tiger
ROALD DAHL
The Giraffe and the Pelly and Me
ROARS
TRY AGAIN SALLY JANE

Dad is a builder.

Dad is a farmer.

Mom is a farmer, too.